O SOUND MIND!

Rajasekhar Ayala

Dedication

This book is dedicated to my dad, who instilled in me an admiration for the beauty of the Telugu and Sanskrit languages at an early age.

Acknowledgment

Ancient wisdom says that to accomplish anything, one needs God's grace and energy in three dimensions – the desire or will to do something, the knowledge as to what and how to do it, and the ability to do it. These are termed Iccha Shakti, Gyana Shakti, and Kriya Shakti in Sanskrit. I am grateful for the early exposure to Telugu literature both at home and in school. The appreciation for this literature resulted in a desire to bring some of the works to a larger audience around the world. In terms of what and how to do, it seemed appropriate to pick one of the most popular poetic works, which is not delegated to scholarly pursuits, but which is commonplace in collective cultural memory. On the ability to do it, I am grateful for the support of my family to embark on this journey, and the digital technology evolution that makes it simpler to compose, edit, publish, and reach out to a broader audience.

INTRODUCTION

This book is a translation of the original work, called "Sumati Shatakam," where Sumati means wise or sound mind, and Shatakam means one hundred (verses). This was written in the South Indian language of Telugu in the 13th century by Baddena Bhupaludu, who was a prince in the Chola empire, which extended its influence to much of present-day Southeast Asia. It has enjoyed enduring popularity among people of all ages, particularly with parents, educators, and children. The verses exhibit a musical quality. Each verse is independent and stands on its own, just like a quote. These verses were written in a simple, commonly used language, making them accessible to everyone. Despite their simplicity, these poems possess remarkable communicative power. Much of the practical wisdom and insights provided by these verses are applicable in modern times in terms of navigating social, political, cultural, and emotional aspects of day-to-day life.

There are several works that provide transliteration of the verses along with English meanings. Also, there were some translations into European languages in the 1900s. However, this is my attempt to bring the original beauty of the verses into a simple poetic form in English, as O Sound Mind! As with the original work, I hope that this appeals to you and that some snippets stick with you to pass on to family, friends, and future generations.

Timeless wisdom is encapsulated as a collection of insightful verses that have resonated across generations and distill the essence of virtuous living, aiming to impart valuable lessons that transcend the boundaries of time and culture.

This poetic translation represents a testament to the enduring power of words in shaping ethical consciousness. Rooted in simplicity, as with the original work, these verses serve as a beacon for individuals seeking guidance on righteous conduct and social values. The language employed in the original work and the translation is deliberately accessible, making it a valuable resource for readers of all ages.

The verses are woven with a musical quality that captures the ear and resonates in the heart. While drawing on the linguistic richness of Telugu, the collection deliberately attempts to ensure, to the extent possible, that the wisdom it imparts is easily grasped by modern readers. As with any translation of poetry, it is not possible to entirely represent the impactful idiomatic expressions, rhyme and meter, wordplay and puns, and cultural nuances and references.

The original work refers to the administrative and political structure of those times and some societal stereotypes. Some themes repeat across the verses, such as work ethic, relationship with an employer, choosing the right friends, perils of association with deceitful people, the transient nature of social relationships, the importance of giving, and the pursuit of the right goals in life. An attempt was made to preserve the intent of the original verses while mapping the context to the current times, where applicable.

The original verses were not confined to the pages of textbooks or literary archives but have become embedded in everyday discourse. It is not uncommon for individuals to quote these gems, illustrating the profound impact they have had on the collective consciousness. Young people encounter these verses during their formative years, imbibing the timeless wisdom that informs their ethical compass. The author hopes that a similar impact can be accomplished with the translated work, forging a connection between classical teachings and the challenges of the modern world.

With God's grace, insights I'll unfold,
Verses of wisdom, your hearts will hold.
As fascinated people, their ears keen,
Listen to good sense, unheard and unseen.
Muse on this, O Sound Mind!

A relative, in times of need, helps not,
A Deity, despite prayers, gives not.
A steed, amid battle, gallops not,
Such ties, for a life that's wise, keep not.
Muse on this, O Sound Mind!

When not given, asked just wages,
Be not glum and serve such masters.
Instead, be free and plow a field,
With some strong bullocks, indeed.
Muse on this, O Sound Mind!

With lavish hope, serve not a Master,
For selfish ends, be not a temple treasurer.
With wicked people, build not rapport,
Without a companion, go not to a forest.
Muse on this, O Sound Mind!

In power's cruel hand, officers who ignore,
To speak pleasant words or silently withdraw;
Corrupted by might, a lifeless guise they wear,
Witnessing such souls, one can only despair.
Muse on this, O Sound Mind!

SCHOOL
BANK
HOSPITAL

A creditor, a doctor, an eternal stream,
A learned teacher who confers wisdom.
Reside in peace where these are present,
Avoid a place where these are not extant.
Muse on this, O Sound Mind!

When starving, any food is a pleasure,
When giving, an unhesitant one is a donor.
Enduring hardship, a real human quality,
Being courageous brings fame to a dynasty.
Muse on this, O Sound Mind!

Food that leaves hunger,
Taste of stale well water.
Goat's milk, a pregnant courtesan,
On this earth, cause aversion.
Muse on this, O Sound Mind!

A mouth that reads not deftly,
That calls not mom for food swiftly,
That invites no siblings, has no worth,
Just like a potter's hole in the earth.
Muse on this, O Sound Mind!

Display of borrowed wealth,
Youthful bride in age near death.
Fool's penance, and a ruler blind to crime,
Sow the seeds of future harm in time.
Muse on this, O Sound Mind!

In life's grand quest, four aims converge,
Morality, wealth, love, and soul's surge.
Without these, why live long years,
Like an iguana, a serpent, or a tortoise?
Muse on this, O Sound Mind!

Wicked hearts dwell in shadows deep,
Try as you may, noble traits don't reap.
Does melting brass anywhere make it gold,
On this earth, no matter what is tried?
Muse on this, O Sound Mind!

To aid the one who aids you,
Common it is, it is what we do.
To aid the hand that dealt a blow,
A skill of heart, a rare gift to show.
Muse on this, O Sound Mind!

Like sugarcane, first sugary, then bland,
At first sweet, friendship with wicked.
Yet, in the end, its flaws are revealed,
Deceit and bitterness unconcealed.
Muse on this, O Sound Mind!

Speak as is appropriate,
At the right time and place.
Not hurting others or getting hurt,
Skill in this is indeed fortunate.
Muse on this, O Sound Mind!

Pick not unripe fruit,
Blame not relatives with fault.
Run not from armed conflict,
Overstep not a Guru's precept.
Muse on this, O Sound Mind!

Quit love that is unreturned,
A distrusting master or a friend.
Foolish is he, who stays on,
When it's time to move on.
Muse on this, O Sound Mind!

Cars come on boats on the water's crest,
Boats pulled by cars on the earth's crust.
In life's dance, the roles may shift,
Rich and poor, fate's hand will lift.
Muse on this, O Sound Mind!

Given in need, small cash seems a lot,
Will save the day, and they forget it not.
Yet once the hour of need dwindles,
Even thousands given seem frivolous.
Muse on this, O Sound Mind!

Giving is the nature of knowledge,
Joining battle is the mark of courage.
Talent is what good poets praise,
Harm is the result of a quarrel's gaze.
Muse on this, O Sound Mind!

In life's design, some sorrows persist,
A lame frog, a sickly serpent,
A wicked spouse, poverty when old.
Fate binds when all else is told.
Muse on this, O Sound Mind!

Anthills rise where ants reside,
Yet serpents in their shelter hide.
Wealth amassed by fools may fleet,
To rulers' hands, its fate complete.
Muse on this, O Sound Mind!

In secrets kept, trust holds its might,
Caution's key in shadows' light.
Confide with care, in whispers low,
For even allies may deal a blow.
Muse on this, O Sound Mind!

In mildness, strength appears to fade,
An elephant's pride, in shadows, laid.
Serpent's bite and scorpion's sting,
If unused, strength loses its fearful zing.
Muse on this, O Sound Mind!

So long as one generously gives,
The Goddess of wealth stays.
Yet once the giving days are over,
Her presence fades forever.
Muse on this, O Sound Mind!

A poet's writings, grace devoid,
A woman's love, emotions unversed.
A hunter skilled, yet prey not killed,
Futile are these, with intents unfulfilled.
Muse on this, O Sound Mind!

A treasurer is one who can say no,
A chief is one who can settle a row.
A king's attendant is one with a firm stance,
A statesman is one who can tell great tales.
Muse on this, O Sound Mind!

In wicked hearts, no friendships bloom,
Fame, once earned, doesn't leave the room.
In lending money, disputes may manifest,
In a lover's heart, love may not persist.
Muse on this, O Sound Mind!

Steeds quenching thirst, go not near them,
Elephants in arrogant frenzy, avoid them.
Bulls in mating season, stay away from,
Mean souls, at any time, keep away from.
Muse on this, O Sound Mind!

In leaking homes, don't live in,
Fighting with a chief, don't revel in.
A biting dog, don't keep at home,
A cheating goldsmith, steer clear from.
Muse on this, O Sound Mind!

Foolhardy are - laughter without reason,
A woman's attire, modesty forgotten,
Sweet dish, with no stuffing in the core,
A wedding with no music to underscore.
Muse on this, O Sound Mind!

Quarrel and blame not a wife,
Leading to a baseless strife.
When lady's tears flow, fortune will part,
In gentle hearts, love finds its start.
Muse on this, O Sound Mind!

In friendship's glow, flaws stay veiled,
Only virtues seen, our thoughts aligned.
When bonds grow weak, truth behold,
Only flaws are seen, as thoughts unfold.
Muse on this, O Sound Mind!

Friendship with an evil soul does bode,
Pathway to a dangerous crooked road.
Just like a cot getting a hard beating,
When a bedbug bites a man sleeping.
Muse on this, O Sound Mind!

In books of love, his knowledge vast,
Handsome allure, a charm to cast.
Though he may be a king with grace,
Only money gets a temptress' embrace.
Muse on this, O Sound Mind!

A son gone astray is not just useless,
Gone is the family name priceless.
Like smut at the edge of sugarcane,
Spoils the sweetness of the whole cane.
Muse on this, O Sound Mind!

In a frugal life, sustenance is bare,
Yet money slips through fickle air.
To rulers, gamblers, and thieves, it flies,
A miser is left with nothing but sighs.
Muse on this, O Sound Mind!

Choose enemies with the utmost care,
More than friends, it behooves to be beware.
Clever foes with the might of power,
May harm your interests forever.
Muse on this, O Sound Mind!

Wealthy shores, kin gather near,
Like frogs to a lake, they draw near.
In numbers vast, they seek to share,
A bounty's weight, they're quick to bear.
Muse on this, O Sound Mind!

On a fake tale of a minister, a king,
Who punishes people without probing,
It is like felling a wish-granting tree,
For the sake of a wood-burning spree.
Muse on this, O Sound Mind!

In wealth's embrace, false kin arrive,
Sweet words mask motives, some connive.
Claiming ties, they seek the gold,
In shadows deep, their schemes unfold.
Muse on this, O Sound Mind!

Charity, pure and kind, graces hands,
Truth adorns kings in their lands.
Morality, an adornment for everyone,
Honor, an ornament for women.
Muse on this, O Sound Mind!

Delays and toil, be ready to endure,
In haste, nothing gets done for sure.
With patience and effort, you can fix,
Targets missed, despite being in a fix.
Muse on this, O Sound Mind!

Your anger is your foe within,
Your calmness shields you in.
Your compassion is your kin,
Your woe hell, your joy heaven.
Muse on this, O Sound Mind!

Penance by an acquaintance,
Son's scholastic advance,
Wife's beauty, backyard tree's cure,
No one ever praises, that is for sure.
Muse on this, O Sound Mind!

Your wealth, a path to joy plenty,
Your poverty, a world of scarcity.
Your death, a world calamity,
Your woman, a heavenly beauty.
Muse on this, O Sound Mind!

Reside not, at a place with no kin,
Avoid grounds of strife and pain.
Or places of discomfort and doubt,
In peaceful homes, joy sprouts.
Muse on this, O Sound Mind!

Worthless is one who doesn't experience,
Taste of betel's spice, and lover's embrace.
Worthless is a lake without lotus,
And a night with no moonlight's touch.
Muse on this, O Sound Mind!

A dog, crowned in grand display,
Elegantly, on a very auspicious day.
On a throne of gold, the dog may sit,
Yet old habits cling, they won't quit.
Muse on this, O Sound Mind!

In a serpent's head, the venom lies,
In a scorpion's tail, the venom lies.
What of a wicked soul in stride,
In every vein, the venom may hide.
Muse on this, O Sound Mind!

Rather than arguing with anyone,
Better to appear moderate, to everyone.
And study texts with insights deep,
Search for life's truths, that you can keep.
Muse on this, O Sound Mind!

Love fades with unkempt grace,
Soiled clothes, untidy face.
Even a lover may go for a cover,
Affection's bond is lost forever.
Muse on this, O Sound Mind!

Hidden wealth, not relished,
To kings or earth, winds up drifted.
Honey stored by bees with care,
Others enjoy what they build there.
Muse on this, O Sound Mind!

Despair not, about things bygone,
Hope not, for lasting love of companion.
Divulge not, royal secrets to a friend,
Only this is the prudent way, you'll find.
Muse on this, O Sound Mind!

Kin's wealth won't boost your fate,
Prosperity rests, on steps you create.
In fortune's dance, your path is paved,
With self-reliance, as your true aid.
Muse on this, O Sound Mind!

Walk not, alone on a desolate road,
Feast not, at an enemy's abode.
Steal not, the wealth of others,
Hurt not, the feelings of others.
Muse on this, O Sound Mind!

Tax collector's grip, a heavy chain,
Gambler's luck may turn to pain.
Goldsmith's wares, a gleaming snare,
Trust with care, in life's affairs.
Muse on this, O Sound Mind!

In responsible leaders, nations thrive,
A judge, lawmaker, chief to guide.
When multiple actors do the same job,
Sow seeds of discord, like an unruly mob.
Muse on this, O Sound Mind!

Politeness oft falls on deaf ears,
Plea to drink milk snubbed with no fear.
Yet threats may get the job done,
Even to get someone to swallow poison.
Muse on this, O Sound Mind!

When power's bounds are overthrown,
The seeds of chaos are surely sown.
With despot's rule, and a baleful feat,
Death may knock, where norms retreat.
Muse on this, O Sound Mind!

Poetry and songs sung to the ignorant,
Will get no appreciative compliment.
Like blowing a conch to hear,
Near a deaf person's ear.
Muse on this, O Sound Mind!

Laugh not, in a large congregation,
With a master, or improper companion.
Mock and jest not, with eminent folks,
Lest a bitter misunderstanding stokes.
Muse on this, O Sound Mind!

In hearts, let enmity not reside,
In poverty, find strength inside.
In congregations, assign no blame,
In infatuation, guard your name.
Muse on this, O Sound Mind!

A good wife does chores with grace,
In bed, a heavenly, sweet embrace.
In deliberation, a guide and counselor,
In serving food, love flows like a mother.
Muse on this, O Sound Mind!

Covet not, others' wealth or women,
Irk not, when others are irksome.
Take on, deeds that bring acclaim,
Wish the best, to all in life's game.
Muse on this, O Sound Mind!

POLICE
POLICE

In adulterous arms, don't stray,
In pursuing wealth, don't lose way.
Find no faults, despite masquerade,
Seek not kin, when fortunes fade.
Muse on this, O Sound Mind!

In wealth's embrace, a man they hail,
Red carpets spread along the trail.
When earnings cease, they keep away,
As with a walking corpse passing by.
Muse on this, O Sound Mind!

Speak not, of things unpleasant to others,
Enter not, a neighbor's home without purpose.
Entangle not, with a woman's shadowed past,
Mount not, a steed, who has arrogance cast.
Muse on this, O Sound Mind!

Mantras whispered, in secret keep,
Strategies crafted, make foes retreat deep.
Seven sins forsaken, let virtues win,
Protect kith and kin, let safety begin.
Muse on this, O Sound Mind!

When water blends with milk,
Looks like it is just milk.
But it sure does spoil the taste,
As friendship with a wicked mate.
Muse on this, O Sound Mind!

Pity not, a wicked man's fall,
A wise man doesn't answer the call.
A scorpion in fire, pull and it will betray,
Sting the rescuer, thanks it won't convey.
Muse on this, O Sound Mind!

At birth's moment, the father's joy is slight,
As recognition builds, his heart turns bright.
When acclaimed, happiness does rebound,
Father's pride, in offspring's praises, found.
Muse on this, O Sound Mind!

To a king, go not with hands bare,
Wife, a god, a son, and a teacher,
To each one, a gift special to share,
In gestures kind, there is a flair.
Muse on this, O Sound Mind!

Traders breathe life into towns,
Water is the life of paddy fields.
The trunk is the life of an elephant,
A woman is the life of opulent.
Muse on this, O Sound Mind!

An honorable man in Fortune's sway,
Forced to seek the mean one's way.
Like an elephant in a shallow stream,
Even in distress, honor would gleam.
Muse on this, O Sound Mind!

Gold's safety lies in not pawning,
Honor in battle lies in not running.
Buy not on credit, as debt may sting,
Befriend not fools, mishaps they bring.
Muse on this, O Sound Mind!

A ruler, without a counselor's advice,
Attempting, in vain, to supervise.
Akin to an elephant without a trunk,
Trying to trumpet, though not drunk.
Muse on this, O Sound Mind!

A kingdom drifts without guidance,
From an adept minister's advice.
Just as a machine fails to work,
When a key joint fails, with a jerk.
Muse on this, O Sound Mind!

Wealth amassed without hearts cared,
Like honey saved, yet never shared.
In selfish vaults, it may smugly reside,
But true worth is when shared worldwide.
Muse on this, O Sound Mind!

Truth is speech's breath,
Good soldiers, a fort's strength.
Honor, a woman's nobility,
Signature, a document's validity.
Muse on this, O Sound Mind!

Engage not, in errands not requested,
Toil not, for a king, without being valued.
Attend not, parties not invited to,
Befriend not, others, if they care not to.
Muse on this, O Sound Mind!

Forgive the flaws in others' doing,
Forget and harp not, after donating.
Yet, forget not, help gotten from others,
In gratitude, remember God's kindness.
Muse on this, O Sound Mind!

With a king, who cares not for you,
Can you secure income and joy?
Groping a house with fingers at night,
Such service is futile, without a light.
Muse on this, O Sound Mind!

Words once spoken echo in the air,
To deny them brings folly and despair.
Support kin, stay away from an irate king,
Into a sinful country, don't go roaming.
Muse on this, O Sound Mind!

Fields bereft of paddy's golden yield,
Lands a ruler's presence fails to shield.
A path traveled without a mate,
Like a cemetery, would be desolate.
Muse on this, O Sound Mind!

Let fields rest in drought, plough not,
To a kin's place in famine, venture not.
Royal secrets, to strangers' ears, reveal not,
A coward at heart, a general, make him not.
Muse on this, O Sound Mind!

In an ocean, a thousand rivers merge,
Yet, sweetness eludes its water's surge.
To a sinner, try imparting wisdom,
Even a thousand ways work seldom.
Muse on this, O Sound Mind!

Listen to everyone's opinion,
Act not hastily, keep the mind open.
Truth from untruth, who screens,
Is a wise person that discerns.
Muse on this, O Sound Mind!

A mouth that spurns betel's bliss,
Doesn't meet the sweetness of a kiss;
A mouth that doesn't sing, melodies amiss,
It lingers like a ditch, an ash-filled abyss.
Muse on this, O Sound Mind!

Mighty serpent meets its end,
By ants, in numbers, being penned.
Likewise, a strong man may tyrannize,
But from pushovers, will face his demise.
Muse on this, O Sound Mind!

530: 1-25
2

Without power, a position has no gist,
Without a position, power lacks might.
Blend the two, a force complete,
Commands obeyed, in power's seat.
Muse on this, O Sound Mind!

Serving under ungrateful leadership,
Uniting with a mate, ignorant of courtship.
Where in friendship's guise, deceit hides,
These are like swimming against nonstop tides.
Muse on this, O Sound Mind!

Education void of exhilaration,
Songs without raga and emotion,
Union cold, desire's flame amiss,
Speech unappreciated, are spiritless.
Muse on this, O Sound Mind!

Jokes lead to discord, in due course,
Happiness leads to sorrow, in due course.
Growth leads to fall, in due course,
Fall in prices leads to rise, in due course.
Muse on this, O Sound Mind!

When it comes, wealth gushes in,
Like water, from a coconut's core within.
When it goes, it departs unseen and silent,
Like wood apple pulp, eaten by an insect.
Muse on this, O Sound Mind!

In discourse, avoid strife with women,
Befriend not and overly engage children.
Noble virtues, let them not wane,
Abuse not, your employer, in reign.
Muse on this, O Sound Mind!

One who finds faults at every turn,
Work not for such a sovereign.
Like a frog resting in the shadow,
Of a serpent's hood in a meadow.
Muse on this, O Sound Mind!

In aiding the wise, a path of honor paved,
Like planting a coconut tree for fruit craved.
Like the nourishing fresh coconut water,
It will bring respect and happiness later.
Muse on this, O Sound Mind!

Undeterred by one who is big,
A virtuous person is strong.
Like on top of a hill-like elephant,
Climbs up and sits a brave mahout.
Muse on this, O Sound Mind!

Lotuses plucked from water's cool embrace,
Wither beneath the sun's relentless blaze.
So too, when one abandons their own space,
Friends turn foes in life's unyielding chase.
Muse on this, O Sound Mind!

~ PEACE ~

About The Author

Welcome to the literary world of Raj Ayala, an aspiring author with a passion for making stories and precepts of ancient wisdom come to life in a way that transcends time and cultural boundaries.

"O Sound Mind!" is Raj Ayala's debut venture into the realm of publishing space. The author hitherto spent much of his time in the world of technology field where ones and zeros and algorithms dance at the edge of innovation. But lo and behold, the binary ballet wasn't enough to contain the creative whirlwind within. Raj Ayala decided to tango with words, to explore the infinite possibilities of storytelling, as the call of the written word became too tempting to resist. The transition to crafting narratives wasn't seamless, but buckle up, dear reader, as you're about to witness the magical transformation from bits and bytes to the wizardry of words in this poetic debut.

www.ingramcontent.com/pod-product-compliance
Ingram Content Group UK Ltd.
Pitfield, Milton Keynes, MK11 3LW, UK
UKHW062001290726
14090UKWH00021B/1330

9 798869 356246